GOING SOLO

TROMBONE

First performance pieces for trombone/euphonium with piano

Erste Vortragsstücke für Posaune/Euphonium und Klavier

Premières pièces de concert pour trombone ou tuba ténor et piano

ALAN GOUT

© 1993 by Faber Music Ltd
First published in 1993 by Faber Music Ltd
Bloomsbury House 74–77 Great Russell Street London WC1B 3DA
Cover illustration by John Levers
Printed in England by Caligraving Ltd
All rights reserved

ISBN10: 0-571-51427-8
EAN13: 978-0-571-51427-4

To buy Faber Music publications or to find out about the full range of titles available please contact your local music retailer or Faber Music sales enquiries:

Faber Music Ltd, Burnt Mill, Elizabeth Way, Harlow, Essex CM20 2HX
Tel: +44 (0)1279 82 89 82   Fax: +44 (0)1279 82 89 83
sales@fabermusic.com   fabermusic.com

1. Going Solo (easy version)

Going Solo (einfache Fassung)   En Soliste (version facile)

Alan Gout

[PIANO TACET]

Maestoso ad lib. ♩ = 72

2. Pavane (from 'Capriol Suite')

Peter Warlock
arr. Alan Gout

Allegretto ma un poco lento ♩ = 80

4

3. O Sacred Head Sore Wounded

O Haupt voll Blut und Wunden   O front sacré tu portes tes blessures

J.S. Bach
arr. Alan Gout

4. Edwardian Evening

Nostalgischer Abend   Soirée Edwardienne

Alan Gout

5. Circus Clowns

Zirkusclowns   *Les Clowns du Cirque*

Alan Gout

6. Ballad

Edvard Grieg
arr. Alan Gout

7. Barcarolle

Alan Gout

8. Serenade

Frederick Delius
arr. Alan Gout

9. Rough and Ready Rag

Alan Gout

10. Boogie for 'bone

Alan Gout

11. Take a Pair of Sparkling Eyes

Arthur Sullivan
arr. Alan Gout

12. Prelude

Präludium   Prélude

Alan Gout

13. Going Solo (hard version)

Going Solo (schwierigere Fassung)   En Soliste (version difficile)

Alan Gout

14. The Old Castle

Das alte Schloß   Le Vieux Château

Modest Musorgsky
arr. Alan Gout

15. Sicilienne

Gabriel Fauré
arr. Alan Gout

16. Blues for 'bone

Alan Gout

from Faber Music

TROMBONE

The *Really* Easy Trombone Book *Alan Gout*

ISBN 0-571-50999-1

First Book of Trombone Solos
 Peter Goodwin & Leslie Pearson

ISBN 0-571-51083-3

Second Book of Trombone Solos
 Peter Goodwin & Leslie Pearson

ISBN 0-571-51084-1

Going Solo *Alan Gout*

ISBN 0-571-51427-8

The Baroque Trombone *Simon Wills*

ISBN 0-571-51723-4

The Victorian Trombone *Simon Wills*

ISBN 0-571-52052-9

Jazzin' About *Pamela Wedgwood*

ISBN 0-571-51053-1

Improve your sight-reading! Grades 1–5
 Paul Harris & John Davies

ISBN 0-571-51077-9

Progressive Jazz Studies *James Rae*

ISBN 0-571-51544-4

FABER *ff* MUSIC